DISABILITY AND THE MEDIA

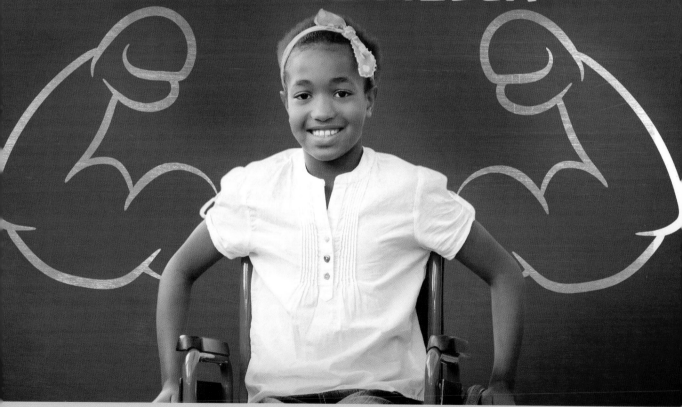

Nicole Evans  **Understanding Disability**

Published in the United States of America by:

Cherry Lake Press
2395 South Huron Parkway, Suite 200, Ann Arbor, Michigan 48104
www.cherrylakepress.com

Reading Adviser: Beth Walker Gambro, MS, Ed., Reading Consultant, Yorkville, IL

Photo Credits: © wavebreakmedia/Shutterstock.com, cover, 1, 7; © Monkey Business Images/
Shutterstock.com, 5; © Kachka/Shutterstock.com, 6; © Rawpixel.com/Shutterstock.com, 8, 9, 14;
© YAKOBCHUK VIACHESLAV/Shutterstock.com, 10; © Iryna Inshyna/Shutterstock.com, 12;
© vladwel/Shutterstock.com, 17

Cherry Lake Press is an imprint of Cherry Lake Publishing Group.

Library of Congress Cataloging-in-Publication Data
Names: Evans, Nicole (Nicole Lynn), author.
Title: Disability and the media / by Nicole Evans.
Description: Ann Arbor, Michigan : Cherry Lake Publishing, [2022] | Series: Understanding disability |
   Includes bibliographical references. | Audience: Grades 2–3
Identifiers: LCCN 2022005378 | ISBN 9781668910719 (paperback) | ISBN 9781668909119 (hardcover) |
   ISBN 9781668913895 (pdf) | ISBN 9781668912300 (ebook)
Subjects: LCSH: People with disabilities—Juvenile literature. | People with disabilities in mass media—Juvenile
   literature. | Mass media and people with disabilities—Juvenile literature. | Disabilities—Juvenile literature.
Classification: LCC HV1568 .H9354 2022 | DDC 362.4—dc23/eng/20220214
LC record available at https://lccn.loc.gov/2022005378

Cherry Lake Press would like to acknowledge the work of the Partnership for 21st Century Learning, a Network
of Battelle for Kids. Please visit http://www.battelleforkids.org/networks/p21 for more information.

Printed in the United States of America
Corporate Graphics

Easterseals is enriching education through greater disability equity, inclusion and access. Join us at www.Easterseals.com.

CONTENTS

WHAT IS MEDIA, AND WHY IS IT IMPORTANT?

Media are the types of communication used to reach large numbers of people. Newspapers, magazines, television, podcasts, TikTok, YouTube, video games, and books are all considered popular forms of media. Millions of people view or interact with them.

There are many different types of media.

Media is powerful because it can be used to educate, entertain, and **influence** large numbers of people around the world. We learn about other cultures, communities, and identities through media.

Have you ever heard the phrase, "With great power comes great responsibility?" Well, that phrase is true

Media helps us learn about the world and the people in it.

Think!

In this chapter we learned that there are many different types of media, including this book that you are reading. Can you think of any other types of media? What kind of media do you watch, listen to, or interact with?

for media, too! Media has power. That is why it is important that the **content** is accurate, **inclusive**, and **representative** of all the people who view it.

REPRESENTATION AND INCLUSION

Have you ever seen someone who looks like you on TV, movies, video games, or other forms of media? It is cool when that happens, right? This is called representation, and representation matters!

Representation is important because it helps other people understand you, your **identity**, and how you might feel. It feels good when people listen to and understand you. Representation of all communities,

Can you think of an example of disability representation in media that you have seen? What did you learn about people with disabilities when you watched or interacted with this content?

9

cultures, and identities in media helps us all grow, learn, and accept each other. Representation helps us all to think differently!

That is why representation and inclusion of people with disabilities in media is important. It helps others understand that people with disabilities are individuals who are just like everybody else and are **valued** members of the community. Disability representation **confirms** our feelings and life experiences. This confirmation allows our voices to be **amplified** in the real world.

Disability representation in media can also inspire the disabled community! For example, imagine that an actor with a disability is playing the role of the U.S. president on a TV show. This would show that it is possible for a person with a disability to be the president. And it is possible!

This example of disability representation might encourage someone with a disability to run for office. Or they might gain interest in politics because they see themselves represented on the screen. That is super cool and shows the power of representation!

Representation matters. Seeing people that look like us trying new things can give us courage to try those same things!

AUTHENTIC REPRESENTATION

When something is **authentic**, that means that it is the real deal. Say you have a real dollar bill and a fake one from a board game. Which can you use to shop at a store? You guessed it! The real authentic dollar bill is the way to go!

This book that you are reading right now is an authentic representation of people with disabilities. That is because I am using my real-life experiences and **perspective** as a person with a disability to write this book about disability. This book is the real deal!

That does not mean that people with disabilities must only write about disability-related subjects. We can write about whatever we want! Instead, it means people with disabilities are the best people to write and **collaborate** with when creating disability-themed content.

Working with groups of different people allows for great ideas to come to the table!

Sometimes characters in a movie or TV show are written to have a disability. It is an authentic representation when the actor playing the role also has a disability. When an actor *without* a disability portrays a character that *is* disabled, that is *not* authentic representation.

That does not mean that actors with disabilities must only play characters that are written as having a disability. We can and should be hired to play every possible character! It is as simple as that.

Ask Questions!

When is the last time that you saw disability representation in media? Did the character have a disability? Is the actor authentically disabled? Ask an adult to help you research online to find the answer!

NOTHING ABOUT US, WITHOUT US!

There is a saying in the disabled community, "Nothing about us, without us!" This means that content *about* disability must always be created *with* people with disabilities.

People with disabilities must always be included as decision-makers in the storytelling process of disability-related media. Remember, representation in media helps millions of people learn about things with which they are unfamiliar. It is important that the information and story-telling is authentic.

Authentic representation helps remove harmful and incorrect information, such as **stereotypes** and **stigmas** of the disabled community. It replaces them with correct information. Authentic representation is what helps to change perspectives. Those changed perspectives help change the world for the better.

Look!

There are so many talented actors, writers, directors, and reporters with disabilities. Research online with an adult! Check out all the cool content created by people with disabilities.

ACCESSIBLE MEDIA AND TECHNOLOGY

Media also involves the type of device or mode that is used to share content. Examples would be iPads, televisions, smartphones, or newspapers. It is important that both the content and the device are **accessible** to people with disabilities. When media is accessible to people with disabilities, this is called accessible media. **Assistive technology** helps to make media more accessible, such as:

- **Audiobooks** are books that you can hear and read with your ears! The book is read out loud by a **narrator**. Audiobooks are cool because they make reading more accessible to people who are blind, have low vision, or have a challenging time reading or concentrating.

- **Audio descriptions** are designed for people who are blind or have low vision. While a movie or TV show is playing, a narrator describes the what is happening on the screen. The person also can hear what the actors are saying.

- **Braille** is a system of raised dots used for reading and writing by people who are blind or have low vision. Braille is read by touching the raised dots with the fingertips.

- **Captioning** is designed for people who are Deaf or hard of hearing. It includes written descriptions on the screen of anything that can be heard, including sound effects. People who have hearing disabilities can read on screen what is being said.

- **Image descriptions** or alt text are pictures you can hear! They are designed for people who are blind or have low vision. Image descriptions work with assistive technology software, such as screen readers, to read the description of a picture out loud. When the picture is described in words, it helps someone with a visual disability experience the picture.

- **Subtitles** are when the speech of the movie or TV show is written on the bottom of the screen. Subtitles are like captioning, but not the same. Subtitles do not always include the same number of descriptions that captioning does. Subtitles help make media more accessible to people who are Deaf, hard of hearing, or are learning a new language.

Create!

Create your own accessible media! Draw a picture, make a short video on your smartphone, or write a short story. How can you make your content more accessible for people with disabilities? Use the assistive technology options above for ideas.

EXTEND YOUR LEARNING

Check out accessible media options!
If you are viewing a movie, experiment with
the control settings and use the captioning,
subtitle, and audio description options.
How do these options make media more
accessible for people with disabilities?
How do you think they could be made
better? Is there anything missing?
Have another idea for assistive
technology? Create it! Advancements in
technology help make the world more
accessible for people with disabilities.

GLOSSARY

accessible (ik-SEH-suh-buhl) easy to get to or to participate in

amplified (AM-pluh-fyed) to be made larger or greater

assistive technology (uh-SIH-stiv tek-NAH-luh-jee) devices that help people with disabilities do things

authentic (aw-THEN-tik) real and genuine

collaborate (kuh-LAH-buh-rayt) to work with someone else on a project

confirms (kuhn-FUHRMS) proves or shows to be true

content (KAHN-tent) something that you can watch, read, listen to, or interact with

identity (eye-DEN-tuh-tee) part of who you are

inclusive (in-KLOO-siv) having a goal to include as many different types of people as possible

influence (IN-floo-uhns) to affect or change something

narrator (NEHR-ay-tuhr) person or character who tells a story

perspective (puhr-SPEK-tiv) the way things are seen from a particular point of view

representative (reh-prih-ZEN-tuh-tiv) serving as an example of something

stereotypes (STEHR-ee-uh-typs) descriptions of someone that are oversimplified, incorrect, and insulting

stigmas (STIG-muhs) long-held and incorrect beliefs about someone or something

valued (VAL-yood) something or someone who is worthy and important

FIND OUT MORE

Books

Burcaw, Shane. *Not So Different: What You Really Want to Ask about Having a Disability.* New York, NY: Roaring Brook Press, 2017.

Burnell, Cerrie. *I Am Not a Label: 34 Disabled Artists, Thinkers, Athletes and Activists from Past and Present.* London, UK: Wide Eyed Editions, 2020.

Websites

Get Involved with Easterseals
https://www.easterseals.com/get-involved
Learn about the different ways you can get involved in increasing opportunities for people with disabilities, from advocacy to volunteering.

YouTube—Easterseals Disability Film Challenge
https://www.youtube.com/c/TheDisabilityFilmChallenge
Check out this page for awesome content created by people with disabilities.

INDEX

ABOUT THE AUTHOR

Nicole Evans is an actress, writer, and disability rights and inclusion activist. She enjoys helping children with disabilities explore their identity and realize their full potential. Born with osteogenesis imperfecta, Nicole is a full-time wheelchair user. Nicole lives in Los Angeles, California.